PENFIELD CENT
ESEA TITLE I

VIP* Series

* Very Important People
IN FOOD SERVICES

**by Dorothy Freeman
Margaret Westover
Willma Willis**

Illustrated by Harold Funston

AN ELK GROVE BOOK

 CHILDRENS PRESS, CHICAGO

Cover photos by Karyl and Joe Youngstrom

Library of Congress Cataloging in Publication Data

Freeman, Dorothy Rhodes.
   V. I. P. in food services.

   (Very important people series: Set IV, The Work world
of personal services; book 1)
   "An Elk Grove book."
   SUMMARY: Simple text and illustrations introduce all
types of jobs connected with food services, including those
of meat cutter, produce clerk, cashier, dishwasher, restaurant
manager, and more.
   1. Food service—Vocational guidance—Juvenile
literature. [1. Food service—Vocational guidance.
2. Vocational guidance] I. Westover, Margaret,
joint author. II. Willis, Willma, joint author. III. Funston,
Harold L. IV. Title.
TX911.2.F73 1976   641.3'0023   75-28503
ISBN 0-516-07462-8

Copyright © 1976 by Regensteiner Publishing Enterprises, Inc.
All rights reserved. Published simultaneously in Canada.
Printed in the United States of America.

1 2 3 4 5 6 7 8 9 10 11 12 13 14 15 R 82 81 80 79 78 77 76

Very Important People Series

Set I   The Work World Of Wheels

Book 1   **V.I.P. who work with CARS, BUSES, AND TRUCKS**

Book 2   **V.I.P. who work with FARM AND EARTH-MOVING MACHINES**

Book 3   **V.I.P. who work with RECREATION VEHICLES**

Set II   The Work World Of Health

Book 1   **V.I.P. ON THE SCENE In Medical Work**

Book 2   **V.I.P. ON THE BACKUP TEAM In Medical Work**

Book 3   **V.I.P. BEHIND THE SCENE In Medical Work**

Set III   The Work World Of Communication

Book 1   **V.I.P. who work with SIGHT AND SOUND**

Book 2   **V.I.P. who CARRY MESSAGES**

Book 3   **V.I.P. who PRINT AND PUBLISH**

Set IV   The Work World of Personal Services

Book 1   **V.I.P. in FOOD SERVICES**

Book 2   **V.I.P. in MAINTENANCE SERVICES**

Book 3   **V.I.P. in PERSONAL AND PROTECTIVE SERVICES**

CONTENTS

The Work World of Personal Services ——————— 8
Choosing Your Work ———————————————— 9
V.I.P. Who Work In Retail Food Stores ————————— 10
   Grocery Baggers————————————————— 10
   Cashiers ———————————————————— 12
   Meat Cutters————————————————— 14
   Meat Wrappers ————————————————— 16
   Produce Clerks———————————————— 18
   Produce Managers————————————————— 18
   Grocery Clerks ————————————————— 20
   Grocery Managers———————————————— 20
   Bakers ————————————————————— 22
   Store Managers ————————————————— 24
V.I.P. Who Work Where Food Is Served———————— 25
   People Who Work In Fast-Service
Shops and Restaurants ———————————————— 26
      Counter Clerks———————————————— 26
      Fountain Workers ————————————— 30

People Who Work In Kitchens	31
Cooks	31
Cooks' Helpers	32
Restaurant Bakers	34
Restaurant Bakers' Helpers	34
Beverage Workers	35
Sandwich Makers	36
Salad Makers	37
Restaurant Meat Cutters	38
Pantry Supervisors	38
Wheelmen	40
Counter Supply Persons	40
Dishwashers	42
Food Assemblers	42
People Who Work In Dining Rooms	44
Waiters/Waitresses	44
Hostesses/Hosts	46
Bus Boys/Bus Girls	46
Restaurant Cashiers	48
Dining Room Supervisors	49
People Who Work In Management and Supervision	50
Restaurant Managers	50
Food Production Managers	51
Menu Makers	52
Directors of Recipe Development	52
Your Future In Food Services	53
More About V.I.P. In Food Services	54
Glossary/Index	55
About the Authors and Illustrator	64

If you work in food services, you could be...

A FOUNTAIN WORKER

A CASHIER

A PRODUCE CLERK

A MEAT CUTTER

A WAITER OR WAITRESS

A DINING ROOM HOSTESS

A FRY COOK

A BAKER

THE WORK WORLD OF PERSONAL SERVICES

Workers in personal services have people-to-people jobs. They prepare and serve food and help people with their appearance, comfort, cleanliness, and safety.

Forecasters say that most future job openings will be for people who serve people. These jobs will be in restaurants, stores, shops, hotels, hospitals, schools, airplanes, and on ships.

This book gives you information about some of the work in food services in stores and restaurants. There are many jobs for beginners. They are called *entry jobs*. In this book they're marked with an **E.** If you begin working while you are still in high school, you will need a *work permit* as well as a *social security number*.

A beginning job in food services can be the first step on a career ladder. You can get on-the-job training and advance to more responsibility and better pay. You may qualify for *scholarships* to help you study further.

CHOOSING YOUR WORK

Most of the jobs in the services put you face-to-face with the people you serve. To be happy in these jobs, you need to like all kinds of people. Most of the time you'll enjoy helping them. Other times you'll need the ability to stay calm and courteous when the people you are trying to help aren't satisfied.

You'll need

▸ to want to help people

▸ to be able to keep track of orders, stock, and supplies

▸ to use small machines and cleaning tools.

The symbols you see above are also printed beside the job descriptions in this book. They stand for

▸ the ability to work well with people

▸ the ability to work with data (facts and figures)

▸ the ability to work well with your hands and tools.

When you see more than one symbol, the first is the most important one for that job. Check your interests with the job symbols to find the job that could suit you best.

Some of the jobs described in this book, such as wheelman and bus boy may seem to be for men only. Women are also welcomed in these jobs by employers.

PEOPLE WHO WORK IN RETAIL FOOD STORES

Food for 200 million people! That's a big order, and it's filled every day of the year in the U.S.A. by more than two-million retail food workers. These hard-working V.I.P. make it possible for you to buy vegetables, meat, and canned and packaged foods near your home.

Many of the workers have jobs behind the scenes, in offices, *warehouses,* and transportation services. The first part of this book describes the jobs of workers who serve customers in stores.

E — GROCERY BAGGERS

There are jobs for beginners in retail food stores. One of these entry jobs is **GROCERY BAGGER.** A bagger is a boy or girl who puts groceries into paper bags or boxes. He learns to pack them so potato chips or eggs don't get crushed.

"May I help you?" the bagger asks the customer. He follows her, pushing the grocery cart, and puts the bags into her car. On his way back to the store, the bagger collects empty carts.

The bagger keeps the check-out counter clean and supplied with bags. Sometimes he carries returned, empty bottles to the storeroom.

An efficient bagger is good for business. Customers return to a store where baggers are pleasant and pack groceries carefully. Sometimes baggers are called *courtesy clerks.*

Many people who manage or own stores began their careers as baggers. A bagger can begin working part time while in high school. He or she learns on the job.

Who can be a bagger? One who

- is at least 16 years of age
- can follow directions
- is courteous and dresses neatly
- can lift and carry bags of groceries.

CASHIERS

The **CASHIER** at a check-out station uses a cash register to record and add up the prices of the customers' purchases. He or she accepts payment and makes change. If there is no bagger, she packs the groceries.

In some stores, the cashier operates an *intercom*. She uses it to ask questions about prices or to call for assistance.

The cashier, sometimes called a *checker*, has to be friendly, fast, and accurate. Cashiers memorize the prices of many items and also use price lists at the register.

A cashier is often the first one to hear customer complaints. She listens courteously and corrects the problem or calls the store employee who can.

When a cashier is not serving customers she restocks small items, such as razor blades and candy, on *convenience racks* near the register.

Supermarket chains usually require an applicant to have a high school education. The *trainee* takes a short course to learn how to operate the company's cash registers and how to work with people. Trainees who do well in their classes progress to on-the-job training at a company store.

A cashier usually completes classroom and on-the-job training in less than six months. He or she must

- be good in math and have a good memory
- be able to operate a cash register
- get along well with other employees and customers
- be able to stand in one place for several hours
- follow company rules about check cashing and customer complaints.

MEAT CUTTERS

Beef, pork, and lamb arrive at large supermarkets in *block-ready* pieces. The **MEAT CUTTER** divides these into roasts, steaks, chops, stew meat, and other cuts. He uses knives, *cleavers,* and power saws. The meat cutter is skilled in working with his hands and has good eye-hand coordination. He has to be strong enough to carry heavy cartons of meat in and out of 30°–50° cold-storage rooms.

There are no special educational requirements for meat cutters, although most employers prefer high school graduates.

Training is available in some high schools and trade schools. It's also offered in *apprenticeship* programs sponsored by the meat cutters *union.* This is on-the-job training that includes some classroom instruction. The apprenticeship lasts for two to three years.

During training, the apprentice meat cutter learns how to estimate the amount of meat on a *carcass* and how to price it to make a profit. His training includes study of the bone and muscle structure of meat animals and how to cut meat.

Meat cutters earn some of the highest wages in the retail food business, and most belong to a union.

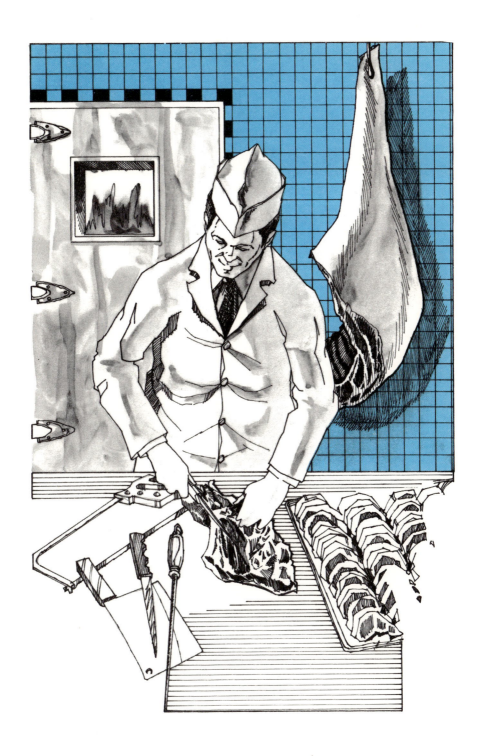

MEAT WRAPPERS

After the meat cutter divides the block-ready meats into smaller cuts, the **MEAT WRAPPER** gets the pieces ready for the display counter.

The wrapper puts a cut of meat into a tray, sometimes called a *boat*. He or she folds plastic wrap over the meat tray. A *conveyor* carries the package into the *shrink tunnel* where heat shrinks and seals the plastic around the package. The package continues on the conveyor to a machine that weighs it and fastens on labels. The labels show the kind of meat, the price per pound, and total price.

Wrappers learn on the job. A wrapper who wants to advance to meat cutter can enroll in a meat cutter apprenticeship program. In a medium-sized supermarket, an apprentice meat cutter often does the wrapping.

Who can work in the meat department of a grocery store? One who is

- physically strong and able to stand for long periods of time
- skillful with meat-cutting tools and likes to work with his hands
- willing to wear an apron and head covering, if required
- courteous and helpful to customers who want special cuts of meat.

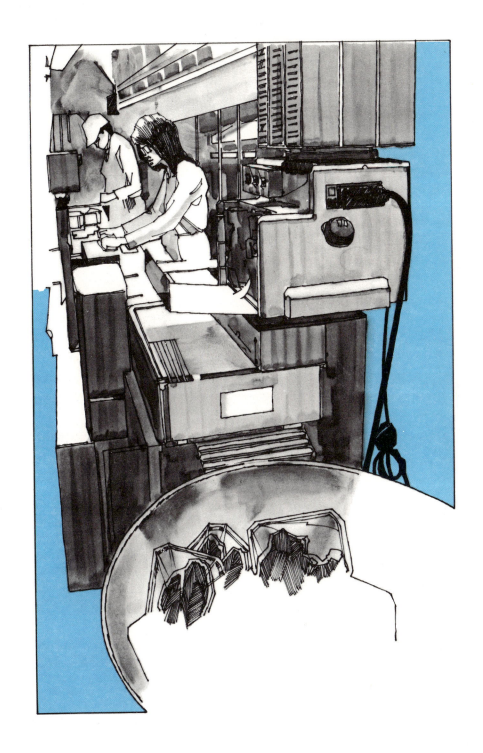

PRODUCE CLERKS

The produce department of a supermarket sells fresh fruits and vegetables. The **PRODUCE CLERK** works there. This V.I.P. begins the day as early as six a.m. and helps unload the trucks that bring boxes of fresh produce to the market. A date is stamped on every box so the clerk knows when the produce arrived in the store.

He or she arranges the *perishable* vegetables on tables called *wet racks* and sprays them with water to keep them fresh and attractive. The clerk inspects the produce, trims off wilted leaves, and moves the oldest items to the top. This V.I.P. arranges dry produce, such as potatoes, onions, and fruits to look attractive. He keeps bags handy for the customers and puts seasonal items on *overflow tables*.

The headquarters of a supermarket chain plans places for all items in the store and decides their prices. The produce clerk makes sure that the arrangement and pricing in his department follow the plan from headquarters. He changes price signs whenever necessary.

PRODUCE MANAGERS

A produce clerk can advance to **PRODUCE MANAGER.** The manager unloads, inspects, and arranges produce, but he has another big job. He or she decides how much of each fruit and vegetable to order. This isn't easy. He has to study the past records of how much apples and lettuce customers have purchased. If he orders too much he may have to sell some at a loss. If he doesn't order enough and runs out, his customers may go to another store to shop.

The produce clerk and produce manager take turns being in charge on each other's days off.

GROCERY CLERKS

The **GROCERY CLERK** handles all the store's stock except meat, produce, and non-food items. This clerk, a man or woman, lifts and cuts open heavy cases of canned and packaged goods. He marks prices on each item with an *ink stamper* or *label gun* and arranges these items on long rows of shelves, called *gondolas*. He makes sure the price on each item matches the price label on the shelf.

Stocking shelves is work that has to be done every day. About 70% of a store's sales are in canned and packaged goods, and shelves get emptied fast.

A very large supermarket may hire grocery clerks to specialize in the dairy, bakery, or *delicatessen* sections.

GROCERY MANAGERS

The head grocery clerk is the **GROCERY MANAGER,** and usually, the assistant manager of the store. He or she is in charge when the store manager is away.

The grocery manager must plan the orders so there is always enough, but not too much, stock on hand for the shelves.

The grocery manager who wants to manage a whole store takes a three-week course to qualify. He can train in a short time because he knows a lot about the jobs in the store and has done almost every one of them at some time.

A grocery clerk or grocery manager is one who

- is well-groomed and has a pleasant personality
- likes people and is able to supervise other employees
- can plan stock orders accurately
- knows math.

BAKERS

Most communities have one or more shops, called bakeries, that specialize in making "home baked" bread and other baked goods. A skilled **BAKER,** man or woman, is usually the owner and head baker. He or she selects recipes, orders supplies, and directs other bakers and helpers who make the baked products in the bakery kitchen.

One baker specializes in baking and decorating cakes and cookies. *Bench hands knead,* roll, cut, form, and place dough in pans to make bread, rolls, and coffee cakes.

In the front of the shop, a *bakery sales clerk* slices the bread loaves on a slicing machine and puts them into bags for customers. This clerk also arranges the baked products in the display counters. She packages items for customers, adds the costs, and rings up the sale on a cash register.

A person may begin a baking career as a sales clerk while still in high school. If he or she wants to be a baker, the first step is to train as an apprentice, beginning as a helper or bench hand. The trainee learns some skills in a few days. Others take months of practice.

Besides these jobs in retail bakeries, there are many more in large industrial bakeries that make thousands of loaves of bread each day. In these large bakeries, workers operate machines that knead, roll, cut, and form the dough. Others tend ovens and the machines that slice and package bread.

Foremen supervise these workers. Computer operators schedule workers, production, and prices. Skilled mechanics keep the automatic machines in perfect working order.

STORE MANAGERS

In a small grocery store, the **STORE MANAGER,** a woman or man, may be the owner. He unloads delivery trucks, stocks shelves, works the cash register, and bags groceries. He may hire help or share the work with other members of his family.

In a large grocery store, the manager hires, trains, and supervises the baggers, cashiers, and clerks. The manager has an office but spends a lot of time in the main part of the store. He sees that clerks keep the store dusted and the shelves stocked. He answers customers' questions and sometimes operates a check-out station during rush hours.

Most managers began their careers as baggers or stock clerks. On these jobs they discovered they liked the food service business and working with people.

To become a grocery chain store manager, a person takes management training classes run by the company. The course lasts about ten weeks. A person with a lot of grocery clerk experience will have a shorter training time.

V.I.P. WHO WORK
WHERE FOOD IS SERVED

Preparing and serving food for people who eat away from home is a large and growing industry. There are many different kinds of jobs wherever food is served and hundreds of kinds of places to work.

Restaurants, hotels, hospitals, schools, industries, drug stores, coffee shops, military bases, airplanes, and ships all serve food. They are located in cities and suburbs, in mountain and beach resorts, along freeways and airlanes, and on the waters of rivers, lakes, and oceans. Variety is the spice of the food service industry!

Would you like to go directly to work after high school? You can get into food service without additional education. Would you rather attend vocational classes, a trade school, a community college, or take four years of advanced education? There are jobs that require all kinds of training.

Good health, special attention to cleanliness, *dexterity*, and willingness to wear uniforms are necessary for food workers. Quickness and pride in offering good food and pleasant service are important to success in any job in the food service industry.

PEOPLE WHO WORK IN FAST-SERVICE SHOPS AND RESTAURANTS

COUNTER CLERKS

E

The duties of a **COUNTER CLERK** in the retail food industry depend on the kind of foods he or she sells.

The *doughnut shop clerk* usually helps to make and frost the doughnuts, as well as sell them.

She mixes the *batter* for the doughnuts according to the shop's own recipe. She tends a machine that drops batter into hot cooking oil and removes the doughnuts when they are golden brown. She arranges these tasty treats on trays for storage and display.

The *dairy store clerk* often works at a drive-in that sells dairy products such as milk, butter, margarine, cottage cheese, and eggs. Many drive-ins also sell fruit juices, bread, and snack foods.

The clerk takes the order at the customer's car window. This V.I.P. has to remember a list of items, such as a half-gallon of milk, two dozen eggs, a loaf of bread, and a bag of potato chips. The clerk sacks the order, rings up the total on the cash register, and puts the package into the customer's car. He takes the money and makes change.

This clerk has to work fast to keep the drive-in traffic moving.

The *fast foodservice clerk* works in a restaurant that specializes in foods such as hamburgers. A *window clerk* takes the customer's order and collects payment for it. In the kitchen at the *grill station,* workers cook meat patties and warm buns. These are put into a *warming bin.* A *bin boy* or *bin girl* assembles the hamburger.

A worker at the *fry station* tends a cooking well of hot oil. She lowers a basket of ready-cut French fries into the oil. When the fries are brown, she lifts the basket and drains it. Using a scoop, shaped to fill a French fries envelope, she fills envelopes and sets them in a holding rack.

A fast foodservice clerk spends most of a working shift at one station but learns to do all the different jobs.

Many counter clerks and fast foodservice clerks begin work while still in high school and learn on the job. Some employers prefer a trainee with some kind of work experience.

Who can work as a counter or fast foodservice clerk? One who

- is dependable about coming to work and arrives on time
- is willing to follow the employer's dress code
- is courteous and likes to serve people
- can figure prices and make change quickly
- has a good memory.

FOUNTAIN WORKERS

A **FOUNTAIN WORKER** is employed by a drug store, ice cream parlor, or snack bar. This V.I.P. takes a customer's order for a soda, sundae, cone, or malt, and makes it on the spot. He or she uses scoops, mixing machines, and soda water and syrup dispensers. He must be a fast worker. While a malt is mixing, he's busy making a banana split or a sundae. In most places he also serves the order, writes up the bill, and collects the money.

In a large restaurant this V.I.P. may prepare fountain foods that other restaurant workers serve. He may have to keep a list of supplies and order more as needed.

Who can be a fountain worker? One who is

- quick and makes every move count
- has a good memory, and can keep several things in mind at the same time
- is clean and neat
- is courteous and likes to serve people.

PEOPLE WHO WORK IN KITCHENS

COOKS

A **COOK** is the boss of the kitchen and the person responsible for the taste and appearance of all food served. He cooks the food, checks the seasoning, plans the size of servings, and adds sauces and decorations to the plates.

Some cooks are well known for their specialties. These may be secret recipes or *ethnic cooking* such as Chinese, French, Italian, English, or Mexican. *Restaurant chains* have recipe books called *formula books*. Cooks use these formula books to make certain that all food is prepared the same way in each restaurant of the chain.

In large restaurants each cook and assistant prepares one type of food such as *appetizers,* soups, salads, breads, or desserts. The cook who supervises all the others is the *chief cook* and is sometimes called a *chef*. He also plans the menu, orders supplies, and hires and trains the other cooks.

Cooks learn their trade through on-the-job training or by taking vocational school or college courses. A beginner can cook, but it takes several years to become a skillful chef.

Who can be a cook? One who

- has a good sense of taste and smell and enjoys preparing food
- has an eye for color and attractive arrangements
- is quick and capable with his hands
- is able to follow recipes

- can give instructions clearly
- knows how to figure costs and quantities for planning menus and ordering supplies
- is in good health and able to stand for most of the working day.

COOKS' HELPERS

A **COOK'S HELPER** prepares food according to the cook's instructions. He or she washes, peels, and cuts vegetables and fruits and gets meat, fish, and poultry ready for cooking. Other duties include weighing and measuring ingredients and stirring and straining sauces and gravies. The helper keeps work surfaces clean, sets oven controls, and adjusts pressure on steam cookers.

This entry job is the first step in learning to be a cook. Some of these jobs are open to people who haven't completed high school.

High school classes in cooking, home economics, and math are useful for a cook's helper. In large cities apprenticeships and other on-the-job training are available.

To advance to cook, the helper needs the ability to follow directions and an interest in food and cooking.

RESTAURANT BAKERS

A restaurant that features "home-baked" bread, rolls, pies, and cakes has a **RESTAURANT BAKER** on its kitchen staff. Most bakers are men, but women are beginning to do this work.

When the baker makes bread, he works the yeast dough with his hands or in a mixing machine. Then he divides the dough into sections for loaves or rolls and sets them in a *proof box* to rise.

The baker who makes bread in a small restaurant usually makes cakes and pies too. In a large restaurant, a *pastry chef* specializes in making pies and cakes. He must be able to decorate cakes as well as bake them.

Bakers learn their skills through vocational classes, trade schools, apprenticeships, or by working as helpers.

RESTAURANT BAKERS' HELPERS

A **RESTAURANT BAKER'S HELPER** brings baking supplies to the kitchen from the store room. The helper weighs and measures ingredients, according to the baker's instructions or a recipe. He mixes them by hand or machine and sets oven heat controls and timers for the baking period.

The baker's helper washes the pots and pans and keeps the work area clean. As the helper gains experience, he is able to take more responsibility for baking jobs.

BEVERAGE WORKERS

In many places where food is served there is a job for a **BEVERAGE WORKER.** This V.I.P., a man or woman, prepares coffee, tea, and hot chocolate for customers. He uses coffeemakers, teapots, and drink mixers.

This worker may serve the beverages to customers or fill the orders given to him by dining room workers. He also keeps utensils clean and polished.

Who can be a beverage worker? One who can

- measure ingredients accurately
- keep utensils and containers clean, inside and out
- keep fresh supplies made
- serve customers courteously
- keep out of the way of fellow workers
- wear an apron and uniform, as required.

E SANDWICH MAKERS

   A **SANDWICH MAKER** learns on the job. The work may be in a restaurant, a public or factory cafeteria, or in a *catering kitchen*.

The sandwich maker, a man or woman, measures and mixes the ingredients for different kinds of sandwich fillings, makes the sandwiches, and often wraps them.

This job requires very fast movements, repeated over and over. Both skill and care are important. A sandwich maker has to keep count of orders for different kinds of sandwiches and keep them separated.

SALAD MAKERS

E

In a day's work, a **SALAD MAKER** cuts, chops, tears, and sections fruits and vegetables. She learns these skills on the job.

This V.I.P. combines crisp, fresh greens or fruit to make salads for customers. He or she also mixes basic ingredients and seasonings to make the dressing that is the "specialty of the house."

Salad makers are quick with their hands and know what looks appetizing and tastes good. They must be willing to wear head coverings and uniforms, if required.

RESTAURANT MEAT CUTTERS

Small restaurants or fast foodservices buy meat supplies already cut to order from a *wholesale meat supplier*. A large restaurant hires a **RESTAURANT MEAT CUTTER** who cuts and trims roasts, chops, and steaks for the restaurant. This worker also prepares poultry, fish, and shell fish for main dishes, soups, and appetizers. He grinds meat and makes sausages.

In very large restaurants each meat cutter may be a specialist, such as a *fish and poultry cleaner* or a *sausage maker*. The person who supervises them is the *head meat cutter*. He also orders meat and keeps records of costs and supplies.

Meat cutters use tools such as knives, cleavers, saws, slicers, and grinders. Some of these tools are electric powered. The meat cutter uses scales to make all servings about the same size. He is responsible for keeping his tools sharp and clean.

A restaurant meat cutter learns his trade in two or three years as a helper or as an apprentice in a meat market.

PANTRY SUPERVISORS

In a restaurant the **PANTRY SUPERVISOR** directs the people who make appetizers, salads, beverages, and sandwiches. Preparing fruit and seafood cocktails, slicing meat and cheese, and making them look good on plates are jobs the pantry supervisor does or oversees. In small restaurants a single pantry person may prepare all beverages and cold foods. In some places he or she may also cook short order breakfasts.

The people who do this work learn their skills through

on-the-job training. Later, they teach others how to be salad or sandwich makers and beverage workers.

Who can be a pantry supervisor? One who is

- quick with his hands and has an eye for detail
- skilled in all pantry work and suited to the fast pace of the job
- able to train and supervise others.

WHEELMEN

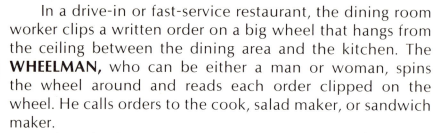

In a drive-in or fast-service restaurant, the dining room worker clips a written order on a big wheel that hangs from the ceiling between the dining area and the kitchen. The **WHEELMAN,** who can be either a man or woman, spins the wheel around and reads each order clipped on the wheel. He calls orders to the cook, salad maker, or sandwich maker.

When the food is ready, this V.I.P. makes sure it is what was ordered, adds the check, and spins the wheel around so a dining room worker can reach the check.

A wheelman gets this job after training in other restaurant jobs. He must be alert, familiar with food serving, and quick in math. The wheelman is often a *short-order cook*.

COUNTER SUPPLY PERSONS

The **COUNTER SUPPLY PERSON** works between the kitchen and the food-serving counter. Most counter supply persons work in *cafeterias*.

This V.I.P. refills steam table containers with hot meats and vegetables and brings salads and desserts to the counter. He or she may decorate food-serving pans or bowls with bits of red pepper or parsley. Wiping up spilled food from the edges of bowls and from counters is also part of this job.

The counter supply person carries clean plates, glasses, silverware, and trays to their places so that these items are always ready for the cafeteria customers.

A counter supply person is

- physically strong and quick
- alert to see where and when he is needed
- able to stand and walk during most of his working day
- acquainted with food preparation and serving.

E DISHWASHERS

Modern machines make dishwashing an easier job than it used to be. Both men and women do this work. The **DISHWASHER** scrapes food from plates and puts dishes into a large dishwashing machine. He adds soap, sets dials that control water temperature and timing, and turns the machine on. It washes the dishes and dries them. This worker removes clean dishes from the machine and puts them away.

The dishwasher hand-washes cooking pots and pans and some other utensils. He keeps stoves, grills, and ovens wiped clean, and also cleans the kitchen floor.

Dishwasher is an entry job. A person doing this work develops skills in handling dishes, becomes quick and efficient, and has a good chance to learn from workers in other kinds of kitchen jobs.

FOOD ASSEMBLERS

A **FOOD ASSEMBLER** packs already-prepared food in trays that are served by airlines, chain restaurants, catering trucks, and school cafeterias. The place where this V.I.P. works is called a commissary kitchen.

Some food assemblers pack meats and vegetables in single servings. Others pack salads, fruit, or sandwiches.

Food assemblers fill cartons with juices and small packages with seasonings or cream. They do much of their work by hand.

The job is a fast, *production-line operation*. The worker usually learns on the job. He or she needs quick, efficient hands and the ability to do the same task correctly again and again.

PEOPLE WHO WORK IN DINING ROOMS

E ## WAITERS/WAITRESSES

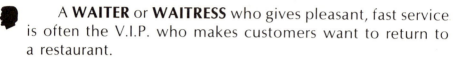

A **WAITER** or **WAITRESS** who gives pleasant, fast service is often the V.I.P. who makes customers want to return to a restaurant.

In a small restaurant she greets customers, leads them to a table, gives out menus, brings water, takes orders, and serves food. The waitress may also make toast and beverages and serve soup and salad.

A waitress usually serves one section of a restaurant. She checks regularly with each table in her section to make sure the customers have the food and service they want. The waitress totals the charges and leaves a *bill* on the table.

When she isn't busy with customers she fills sugar bowls, salt and pepper shakers, and napkin holders. A worker who does all these jobs is called a *combination person*. In large restaurants these jobs are shared by several workers.

Waitress or waiter is an entry job in small restaurants and cafes. Larger restaurants require previous experience and give additional on-the-job training.

Who can be a waitress or waiter? One who

- is able to take food orders accurately
- can stand and walk for most of an eight-hour shift
- can follow directions and is alert
- is neatly groomed and willing to wear a uniform
- can do math
- enjoys serving people and gets along well with fellow employees.

HOSTESSES/HOSTS

When you go into large restaurants, the person who greets you is the **HOSTESS** or **HOST.** This V.I.P. leads you to a table that is ready for customers and presents the menu.

She is the traffic director and tries to seat people at tables or booths they prefer. At the same time, she tries to place them so the waiters have an equal number of customers to serve.

The hostess is usually the one who receives telephoned reservations for meals. She writes down the name, the number of people, and the hour they wish to be served. The hostess must honor reservations, but if the customers are late, she may assign them to a table other than the one they asked for.

Sometimes people wait in the restaurant's entry hall or the bar. The hostess calls them on the intercom when their table is ready.

Hostess or host is a job for a person who likes dealing directly with all kinds of people.

BUS BOYS/BUS GIRLS

The **BUS BOY** or **BUS GIRL** carries used dishes from the restaurant dining room to the kitchen. He or she also brings stacks of clean plates, cups, and saucers from the kitchen as they are needed in the dining area. When he isn't carrying dishes, a bus boy may refill customers' water glasses and coffee cups or refill table containers with sugar, salt, and pepper.

In some restaurants he clears and wipes tables and sets them with clean silverware and napkins. In a restaurant that uses table cloths, he changes these when they are soiled.

When food or drinks are spilled, the bus boy does the cleanup.

He may keep the service counter supplied with ready-made salads and desserts for the waitresses and waiters to pick up.

The bus boy learns on the job. This is a good entry job because it offers a chance to see how a restaurant operates, both in the kitchen and in the dining room. An alert, capable bus boy can advance to waiter or short-order cook. With training he could progress to manager or head cook, depending on his interests.

RESTAURANT CASHIERS

 In many restaurants, a **RESTAURANT CASHIER** is stationed at the cash register. His or her main duties are to check the addition on customers' bills, accept payments, and complete *credit card forms*. She may accept money directly from the customer or make the change for a waiter or waitress.

The cashier must be accurate and fast in making change. She may keep some records for the restaurant, such as the number of meals served in a day.

If a customer complains when he pays the bill, she discusses the problem courteously and makes a change on his bill if necessary.

In a cafeteria where customers serve themselves and carry trays of food past the cash register, the cashier may be called a *food checker*. To ring up the total and make correct change, she must know the price of each item the customer puts on his tray.

Since all customers must pass the checking station, the food checker cannot leave her cash register unless another checker takes her place.

Who can be a cashier or food checker? One who

- is good in math and can make change quickly
- is able to get along well with customers and other employees
- has a good memory
- is well groomed at all times.

DINING ROOM SUPERVISORS

In a large restaurant, a **DINING ROOM SUPERVISOR** is in charge of the other dining room workers. Sometimes this V.I.P. is called a head waiter, head waitress, or *foodservice supervisor*.

She does many jobs that make the dining room run efficiently. She trains waiters, waitresses, and bus boys. She plans their working shifts so there is plenty of help during busy times, and tries to divide the work fairly among the dining room employees.

A supervisor needs to understand the jobs of all other workers in the dining room. Experience as a waiter or waitress can help. She also needs ability to direct people tactfully. A capable supervisor might advance to assistant manager.

PEOPLE WHO WORK IN MANAGEMENT AND SUPERVISION

RESTAURANT MANAGERS

The **RESTAURANT MANAGER** directs all the employees and knows every job he asks them to do.

In a medium-sized restaurant the manager works directly with the head cook in the kitchen and with the dining room supervisor. He consults about menu planning, food purchases, and food service. In a large restaurant he assigns some of this work to an assistant and other members of his staff.

It's popular to decorate a restaurant using a theme, such as "Old West," "South Pacific," or "Shipboard." An owner-manager can plan any theme he wants, but the manager of a chain restaurant has the decorations planned for him.

Any restaurant has to serve customers well and keep them pleased with the food so they will return often. It is the manager's job to see that his restaurant sells enough meals to make enough money to stay in business.

The manager may have been a waiter or a supervisor who was promoted. Or he may have learned the work in community college courses. Most of the time a manager works as a manager trainee before he takes full responsibility for the restaurant.

FOOD PRODUCTION MANAGERS

The **FOOD PRODUCTION MANAGER** is in charge of the kitchen staff and food preparation for a large restaurant. He directs and plans with the cooks and kitchen staff so that they work well together and don't waste food or time. He is sometimes called the *executive chef*.

The money collected for restaurant meals has to pay for the food and the wages of all employees and provide a profit for the owner. The food production manager knows how to prepare and serve good meals at the lowest cost. His training includes courses in cost control and food management at a community or four-year college.

MENU MAKERS

The **MENU MAKER** in a large restaurant or chain of restaurants, has a full-time job planning the kinds of meals and foods the restaurant serves. She checks frequently with the manager to learn what customers order most often. She plans new and different foods to add to the menu.

This V.I.P. can be a man or woman and should have a college degree in *dietetics* or *food and nutrition*.

DIRECTORS OF RECIPE DEVELOPMENT

Large chains of restaurants need college graduates who can work in testing kitchens experimenting and developing new recipes. **DIRECTOR OF RECIPE DEVELOPMENT** is an interesting and creative job. A man or woman who wants to work in this part of foodservice studies food preparation, menu planning, dietetics, food-cost accounting, and purchasing.

There are many other administrative jobs in the food service industry. The necessary skills and information can be learned in college classes.

To prepare for an administrator's job, a person usually works at least three summers in restaurants or hotels at jobs ranging from bus boy to assistant manager. In the winter months his college classes include restaurant administration, institutional management, dietetics, home economics, business administration, and psychology.

Graduates of four-year colleges have a wide choice of jobs. They may work in restaurants, in large industrial and military food preparation centers, in hospitals, and school food services.

YOUR FUTURE IN FOOD SERVICES

"You can start as a part-time beginner and advance to a better job." That sounds like an old success story that doesn't happen any more. But in the food services, it is true that you can learn on the job and move up to more pay and responsibility.

There will be new kinds of jobs in supermarkets for people who can operate electronic equipment. Many markets have computerized cash registers now. In the future, *magnetic scanners* will check out purchases. A computer will total the cost and put the amount on the customer's credit card.

The outlook for restaurant jobs is good because people always look for new restaurants where they can eat delicious and unusual foods. The future is especially promising for waiters, waitresses, kitchen helpers, and skilled cooks.

The food processing industry which makes such foods as catsup, TV dinners, and breakfast cereal also hires thousands of workers. New ways of processing and packaging foods are developed every day and workers are needed. In the U.S.A. more than 50-million loaves of bread are sold each day. That's enough to make a bread-loaf belt around the earth, and it means job opportunities for bakers and bakers' helpers.

Since no one can get along without food, the food service industry will continue to grow, improve, and need new ideas and new workers. If you want to study more about it many scholarships are available to help you. Your skills and ideas and interests may be right for this important industry.

MORE ABOUT V.I.P.
IN FOOD SERVICES

For entry jobs, see the managers of grocery stores and restaurants near your home.

Amalgamated Meat Cutters and Butcher Workmen of North America, 2800 N. Sheridan Road, Chicago, IL 60657

American Bakers Association
1700 Pennsylvania Ave., NW, Washington, D.C. 20006

American Culinary Federation Educational Institute
1008 Woodside Road 201, Redwood City, CA 94601

American Hotel and Motel Association
888 Seventh Ave., New York, N.Y. 10019

American Meat Institute,
59 E. Van Buren St., Chicago, IL 60605

Associated Retail Bakers of America
731 W. Sheridan Rd., Chicago, IL 60613

Club Managers Association of America
5530 Wisconsin Ave., Washington, D.C. 20005

Council of Hotel, Restaurant and Institutional Education,
1522 K St., NW, Washington, D.C. 20005

Culinary Institute of America,
P.O. Box 53, Hyde Park, NY 12538

Food Service Executives Association
508 IBM Building, Fort Wayne, IN 46805

International Chefs Association
121 West 45th St., New York, NY 10036

Meat Packers and Stockyards Administration, Division of Personnel, Office of Management Services, U.S. Dept. of Agriculture, Washington, D.C. 20250

National Association of Retail Grocers
360 N. Michigan Ave., Chicago, IL 60601

National Association of Wholesale-Distributors
1725 K St., NW, Washington, D.C. 20006

National Institute for Foodservice Industry
120 S. Riverside Plaza, Chicago, IL 60606

National Restaurant Association, Director of Education
1530 N. Lake Shore Drive, Chicago, IL 60600

National School of Meatcutting, Inc.,
Toledo, Ohio 43600

The Statler Foundation, Statler Hilton Hotel,
Suite 508, Buffalo, NY 14202

GLOSSARY / INDEX

Note Some of the words defined in this glossary have several meanings. The meanings described here are the ones used in this book.

PAGE

appetizers — **31** small, tasty snacks served before a regular meal

apprenticeship — **14** the period of time an apprentice spends working with a skilled person to learn a trade from him

baker — **22** a person who mixes ingredients and bakes bread, pies, and cakes

bakery sales clerk — **22** a person who sells bread, cakes, and pies

PAGE

batter 26 a mixture of ingredients, deep-fat-fried, to make doughnuts

bench hand 22 a person who helps the baker in the kitchen

beverage worker 35 a person who makes coffee, tea, hot chocolate, and other beverages in a restaurant

bill 44 a slip of paper that shows what the customer owes the restaurant

bin boy/bin girl 28 a person who assembles parts of a hamburger in a fast-service restaurant

boat 16 a small, plastic or paper tray used to hold a cut of meat

block-ready (meat) 14 a large piece of meat ready to be cut into smaller pieces for sale

bus boy/bus girl 46 a person who clears away soiled dishes and prepares tables for the next customers

cafeteria 40 a self-service restaurant

carcass 14 the body of an animal

cashier 12 a person who adds up a bill, collects money, and makes change

catering kitchen 36 a place where people prepare and package food to be served at another location

56

PAGE

checker 12 a cashier in a grocery store

chef 31 a head cook in charge of the restaurant kitchen

chief cook 31 a head cook or chef

cleaver 14 a heavy, wide-blade chopper with a large handle

combination person 44 a worker who takes orders, serves food, and keeps salt and pepper shakers, sugar bowls, and napkin holders filled

convenience rack 12 a shelf for small items near the check-out station in a grocery store

conveyor 16 a moving belt or platform that carries items from one place to another

cook 31 a person who prepares and cooks food

cook's helper 32 a person who assists a cook

counter clerk 26 a person who sells or serves ready-to-eat food directly to the customer

counter supply person 40 a worker who brings supplies of food and dishes from the kitchen to the food service area

courtesy clerk 10 a grocery bagger

57

PAGE

credit card form   **48** a printed form that can be completed with a credit card and used instead of money

dairy store clerk   **26** a person who sells products in a dairy store or drive-in

delicatessen   **20** a part of the store where cheese and cold meats are displayed

dexterity   **25** quick, skillful use of hands and fingers

dietetics   **52** the study of food needed for health

dining room supervisor **49** a person who plans and oversees the work of the restaurant dining room employees

director of recipe development   **52** a person who makes up recipes by experimenting and testing

dishwasher   **42** a worker who hand-washes large pots and pans and operates a machine that washes dishes

doughnut shop clerk   **26** a person who makes and sells doughnuts in a shop

entry job   **8** a job for a beginner

ethnic cooking   **31** cooking of one nationality or another

executive chef   **51** a food production manager

PAGE

fast foodservice clerk 28 a person who cooks or serves food that takes a short time to prepare

fish and poultry cleaner 38 a person who prepares fish and poultry for cooking

food and nutrition 52 a study of the foods most nourishing to the body

food assembler 42 a person who assembles and packages foods to be served at another location

food checker 48 a cashier in a cafeteria who figures the price of the customer's food and collects the money

food production manager 51 a person in charge of all kitchen staff and food preparation in a large restaurant

foodservice supervisor 49 a dining room supervisor

foreman 22 a person who supervises other workers in an industrial bakery

formula book 31 a book of recipes used by cooks who work for a large chain of restaurants

fountain worker 30 a person who makes and serves ice cream dishes and various drinks

fry station 28 the place where French fries are made in a fast-service restaurant

gondola 20 a row of shelves used to display items for sale

PAGE

grill station   **28** the place where fried foods are prepared in a fast-service restaurant

grocery bagger   **10** a person who puts groceries into sacks or boxes for customers

grocery clerk   **20** a person who takes grocery items out of large containers, marks their prices, and puts them on display shelves

grocery manager   **20** a person who supervises workers and directs activities in the store's grocery section

head meat cutter   **38** a person in charge of meat cutting in a restaurant

host/hostess   **46** a person who greets the restaurant's customers and seats them at tables

ink stamper   **20** a small, hand-held device that stamps prices on grocery store items

intercom   **12** an electronic system for communicating inside the store

knead   **22** to press, fold, and work dough by hand

label gun   **20** a small, hand-held device that sticks price labels on grocery store items

magnetic scanner   **53** an electronic device that reads the price marks on grocery items

PAGE

meat cutter   14   a person who cuts meat into pieces suitable for cooking

meat wrapper   16   a person who packages meat to be sold in stores

menu maker   52   a person who plans the menus for a large restaurant chain

overflow table   18   a display table for special items in the produce department

pantry supervisor   38   a person who oversees the workers who prepare salads, sandwiches, and beverages in a restaurant

pastry chef   34   a baker who specializes in making pies and cakes

perishable   18   fresh for a short time, easily and quickly spoiled

produce clerk   18   a person who works in the fruit and vegetable department of a grocery store

produce manager   18   a person who supervises the clerks who work with fruit and vegetables

production-line operation   42   assembly line work where each person does a different part of a job

proof box   34   a container where bread dough is placed to rise

PAGE

restaurant baker   **34** a cook who prepares bread and pastries

restaurant baker's helper   **34** a person who helps the baker by getting, measuring, and mixing ingredients

restaurant cashier   **48** a person who accepts payment from the customer

restaurant chain   **31** a group of restaurants, all under the same top management

restaurant manager   **50** a person who is responsible for all the work and workers in a restaurant

restaurant meat cutter   **38** a restaurant worker who cuts meat into pieces for cooking

salad maker   **37** a person who prepares dressings and the fruits and vegetables for salads

sandwich maker   **36** a person who prepares fillings and makes different kinds of sandwiches

sausage maker   **38** a person who mixes meat and seasonings to make sausage

scholarship   **8** money awarded to students to help them complete their education

short-order cook   **40** a person who cooks food that takes a short time to prepare

shrink tunnel   **16** a machine that automatically seals plastic wrapping around meat

62

PAGE

social security number 8 an official identification number assigned by the federal government to anyone who applies for it

store manager 24 a person who supervises all other workers in the store

trainee 12 a person in training for a job

union 14 an organization of workers

waiter/waitress 44 a person who takes a customer's order for food and serves it

warehouse 10 a building where goods are stored

warming bin 28 a place to keep food warm until it is served

wet rack 18 a display place where vegetables can be sprayed with water

wheelman 40 a person who takes the food order from an overhead wheel and passes the prepared food to a waiter

wholesale meat supplier 38 a person or company that sells meat to stores and restaurants

window clerk 28 the person who takes orders and collects payment in a fast-service restaurant

work permit 8 permission for a young person to hold a job while he or she is still in high school

About the Authors and Illustrator

Dorothy Rhodes Freeman

Dorothy Freeman, an educator who has taught all grades from kindergarten to graduate college classes, is now the principal of an elementary school. She writes when she needs books and can't find them in print. Her books have included texts on map-reading, books for children with a Mexican heritage, and the V.I.P. series.

Her active life revolves around a grown-up family, outdoor hobbies, and teaching a class in children's literature at Chapman College in Orange, California.

Margaret Westover

With a B.A. in Social Sciences and a Masters Degree in Psychological Counseling, Margaret Westover is an employment counselor for the State of California. She has served in many work worlds. As a child, she picked cotton and has been a medical assistant, teacher, mail messenger, journeyman layout mechanic, librarian's aid, and social worker. Her hobbies are camping, flying, raising dogs, and writing about her experiences.

Willma Willis

Willma Willis lives on a farm in central California at the western base of the Sierra Nevada Mountains. A native Californian, she began writing for magazines at 19, an activity which was frequently interrupted, as well as enhanced by marriage, rearing three sons, and community involvements. Free-lance writing efforts since the mid 60s have included magazine articles, public relations, and children's books.

Harold Funston

Native Californian Harold Funston is a graduate of the Art Center College of Design at Los Angeles. As a free-lance artist he has produced set designs and on-air art for a television station. He also does ad illustrations for airline companies and style illustrations.

He loves to ski and collect old books, antiques, and "neat old stuff."